Jan Mark

Shipwrecks

Illustrated by Roger Stewart

OXFORD
UNIVERSITY PRESS

This book belongs to

OXFORD
UNIVERSITY PRESS

Great Clarendon Street, Oxford OX2 6DP

Oxford University Press is a department of the University of Oxford.
It furthers the University's objective of excellence in research, scholarship,
and education by publishing worldwide in

Oxford New York

Athens Auckland Bangkok Bogotá Buenos Aires
Cape Town Chennai Dar es Salaam Delhi Florence Hong Kong Istanbul
Karachi Kolkata Kuala Lumpur Madrid Melbourne Mexico City Mumbai
Nairobi Paris São Paulo Shanghai Singapore Taipei Tokyo Toronto Warsaw

with associated companies in Berlin Ibadan

Oxford is a registered trade mark of Oxford University Press
in the UK and in certain other countries

Hardback ISBN 0-19-910630-4
Paperback ISBN 0-19-910631-2

1 3 5 7 9 10 8 6 4 2

Printed in Spain by Edelvives.

Contents

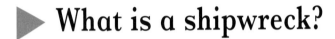 What is a shipwreck?

Any ship can be wrecked. There is no such thing as an unsinkable ship.

Some ships run aground in water that is too shallow. They can catch fire or capsize, turning over in the water. Most wrecks happen when one ship collides with another.

People thought
that the *Titanic* was
unsinkable. But she hit an
iceberg on her maiden
voyage in 1912, and sank.

Everyone knows about the
Titanic but that kind of
accident is very rare.

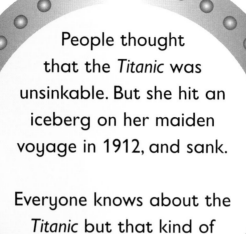

The very first ships were rowed with oars or driven by wind in their sails. Even the fastest ships were not very fast.

oil tanker

The great sailing ships could move at high speed. Ships driven by engines are faster still, and they do not have brakes. They can not just stop moving. Their engines are put astern. This is like putting a car's gears into reverse, but even so, an oil tanker might take twenty minutes to stop.

Did you know ...
You can not park a ship by stopping its engine or taking down its sails. Unless it is anchored it will drift away. The anchor is a heavy weight on the end of a chain.

Careless drivers cause road accidents. Careless sailors can cause shipwrecks, but these do not happen only at sea. There have been two terrible wrecks on the River Thames, right in the middle of London.

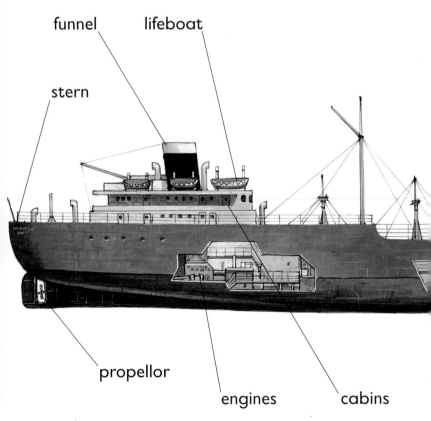

funnel
lifeboat
stern
propellor
engines
cabins

Did you know . . .
The back of a ship is called the stern.
The front is the head. So, ahead means
forwards. Astern means backwards.

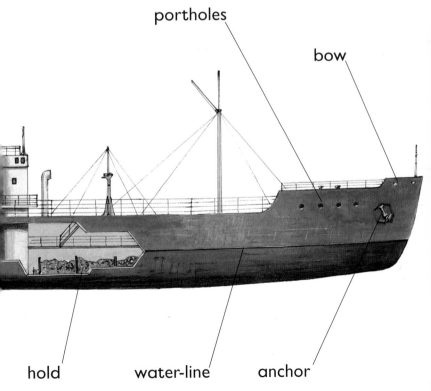

portholes

bow

hold   water-line   anchor

The *Flying Enterprise*

The *Flying Enterprise* was a cargo ship, crossing the Atlantic. The waves were rough, the cargo shifted and the ship began to list. The passengers and crew were rescued but Captain Carlsen stayed with his ship.

The *Flying Enterprise* took sixteen days to go down and no one died. The *Titanic* sank in three hours and 1500 people were lost.

A tugboat, the *Turmoil*, came to help. One of the crew, Mr Dancey, leaped from the *Turmoil* to the deck of the *Flying Enterprise*. The tug tried to tow the ship to safety but the towline broke. Carlsen and Dancey were rescued by the *Turmoil*.

▶ When the wind blows

Ships have been wrecked only a little way from shore. They did not hit rocks or icebergs, they simply capsized.

Some ships capsize because they are overloaded. Once, more than 4000 people were drowned when a ferryboat sank. It was not built to carry so many people.

Sometimes a ship capsizes because it is badly designed. The *Wasa* sank in Stockholm harbour. She was very top-heavy, more like a floating castle than a ship. This was bad design. All it took was one gust of wind to capsize her.

the *Wasa*

The same thing happened to King Henry VIII's warship, the *Mary Rose*.

Ships like this fired cannons at the enemy. The cannon were fired through doors called gun ports.

Mary Rose sailed into battle with her gun ports open. She was overloaded with cannon and soldiers as well as her crew. When she turned to fire, the wind caught her sails. The ship heeled over. The sea rushed in at the open gun ports and *Mary Rose* went down in sight of land.

the *Mary Rose*

▶ Sunken treasure

Mary Rose and *Wasa* have been brought back up from the seabed.

It is not easy to raise a sunken ship but often divers can salvage the cargo. There are many stories of treasure found in wrecks. It may be jewels, silver coins, golden plates, or even ingots.

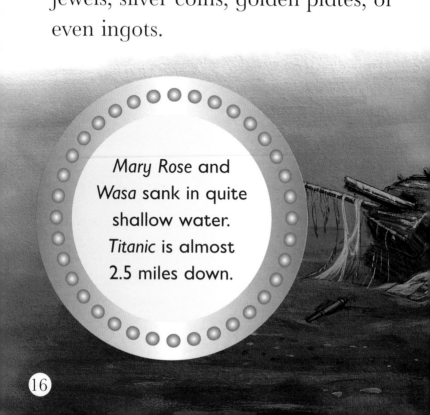

Mary Rose and *Wasa* sank in quite shallow water. *Titanic* is almost 2.5 miles down.

In the Mediterranean Sea is a wreck that is 4500 years old. Not much of the wooden ship is left but divers found the cups, jugs and cooking pots that she carried. Sometimes divers find skeletons.

Did you know . . .

On Lake Ontario, in Canada, a ship once sank with a cargo of dried peas. People called the place Soup Bay.

The lighthouse

In fog or darkness sailors can not always tell how close they are to land. Then a ship may run aground on rocks or a sandbank. Sandbanks are especially dangerous because they do not stay in the same place. They move with each tide.

People have always used lights to warn ships away from dangerous coasts. Once they lit signal fires on the shore or in buildings. These buildings were the first lighthouses.

This is the lighthouse the Romans built at Dover, nearly 2000 years ago. You can still see the remains of it today.

Once, all lighthouses had men living in them to look after the lights. Now they are mostly automatic.

The Stevenson family built ninety-seven lighthouses round the coast of Scotland. Their lighthouses saved thousands of lives. They still do.

Skerryvore lighthouse

Did you know ...
Robert Louis Stevenson was no good at building lighthouses. He became an author instead and wrote books about shipwrecks and treasure.

To the rescue

Some warning lights are in special ships, anchored offshore. Some lights are on buoys.

But even with all these warnings, ships are still wrecked along coasts. When a ship is in trouble it puts out a distress call. Air-sea rescue services may send out a helicopter, or a lifeboat will be launched.

Lifeboats are built to stay afloat in the roughest seas. But sometimes even a lifeboat is wrecked and the crew is drowned.

Many countries have lifeboat services. The British one is the Royal National Lifeboat Institution. In the RNLI the men and women in the crew are volunteers.

► War and peace

In wartime ships are wrecked
on purpose.

In the days when ships were rowed
with oars they would ram each other.

Ships like the *Mary Rose* fired their rows of cannon at the enemy.

If a ship was built of wood the best way to put it out of action was to set it on fire. A ship made of steel plates must be blown up, or holed below the water-line. Once the engine room is flooded a ship is helpless.

HMS *Glorious* was an aircraft carrier. In World War II she was sunk with all her planes on board.

Two destroyers went down with her and more than 1500 men died in the three ships.

HMS *Glorious*

This was a terrible loss of life,
but not many people remember
HMS *Glorious*. Why does everyone
remember the *Titanic*?

Why does everyone remember the *Titanic*?

Perhaps because *Titanic* sank in peacetime. *Glorious* was a warship with a fighting crew.

Perhaps because *Titanic*
was so enormous.

Perhaps because people thought
Titanic could not sink. There is no
such thing as an unsinkable ship.

▶ Glossary

This glossary will help you to understand what some important words mean. You can find them in this book by using the page numbers given below.

aircraft carrier An aircraft carrier is a very large ship with a flight deck where aeroplanes can land and take off. **26**

cargo Things that are loaded on to a ship and carried by it are called the cargo. **10, 16, 17**

distress call This is a signal asking for help. Once ships fired rockets. Now they use radios. **22**

ferryboat A ferry makes short journeys backwards and forwards between two seaports or across rivers. **12**

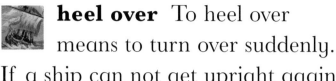 **heel over** To heel over means to turn over suddenly. If a ship can not get upright again it will capsize. **15**

 HMS Ships in the Royal Navy are called HMS – His or Her Majesty's Ship. **26, 27**

 ingot An ingot is a bar of metal, like a brick. **16**

list A ship is listing when it leans to one side. **10**

maiden voyage The maiden voyage is the first journey made by a ship. **5**

 salvage When you salvage something you save it. The thing you save is called salvage, too. **16**

Reading Together

Oxford Reds have been written by leading children's authors who have a passion for particular non-fiction subjects. So as well as up-to-date information, fascinating facts and stunning pictures, these books provide powerful writing which draws the reader into the text.

Oxford Reds are written in simple language, checked by educational advisors. There is plenty of repetition of words and phrases, and all technical words are explained. They are an ideal vehicle for helping your child develop a love of reading – by building fluency, confidence and enjoyment.

You can help your child by reading the first few pages out loud, then encourage him or her to continue alone. You could share the reading by taking turns to read a page or two. Or you could read the whole book aloud, so your child knows it well before tackling it alone.

Oxford Reds will help your child develop a love of reading and a lasting curiosity about the world we live in.

Sue Palmer
Writer and Literacy Consultant